From Soul Boy to Soul Man

The unfolded story of 25 years of Cali-R

By
Sid Hudson

From Soul Boy to Soul Man
Copyright © Sid Hudson (2022)

The right of Sid Hudson to be identified as the author of this work has been asserted by the author in accordance with sections 77 and 78 of the Copyright, Designs, and Patents Act 1988.

First Published in 2022

Book cover design and Book layout by:
Hinton Media Limited
www.Hinton-Media.com

All rights reserved. No part of this book may be reproduced or translated in any form or by any means, electronic or mechanical, including photocopying, recording or by any information storage and retrieval system without written permission from the author.

Contents

Chapter 1
The Boy From The Bush   04 - 18

Chapter 2
The birth of the Cali-Reunion   19 - 37

Chapter 3
A photo chapter looking back at the Cali- 38 - 86
R events from the start till now

Chapter 4
Life around the Cali-R   87 - 109

Chapter 5
Cali-R going forward   110 - 113

INTRODUCTION

Starting with the "why" is a concept that, according to Simon Sinek, the American author and inspirational speaker, provokes reason behind an organisation. It is also part of a bigger framework, including the "what" and the "how". He said: 'If you ask yourselves these questions, you create the golden circle, which can lead to better decision-making and understanding.' Although Cali-R is an event and not a corporation, it is still a concept that I would like to use to create an understanding of how this book was written. So, here we go:

Why?
My passion for Soul Music was born when I first heard Otis Redding as a teenager. This shaped my career and led to the creation of the Cali-R reunion and all that followed.

How?
For the past 25 years, I, the Cali-R team and the Cali-R crowd have come together once or twice a year and immersed ourselves in nights of pure Motown, Soul and Reggae music, often including performances from legendary artists of their

youth in the 70s. In addition, there are smaller events dotted around Bedfordshire, where the enthusiasm and input of the crowds are the same.

What?
Cali-R is a Motown, Soul and Reggae event hosted in the Luton and Dunstable area by Sid Hudson and the Cali-R team.

Inside this book, you will read the unfolded story of Cali-R. The book is written by me, Sid Hudson, and covers the beginning of Cali-R, starting with a short story of my life, and how, as a teenage boy, the spirit of Soul Music touched my life after I listened to "These Arms Of Mine" by Otis Redding. You will then go on a journey and see how I went from teenager to DJ; to DJ promoter; and then to presenting Cali-R events, which have thrived for 25 years. 'Do you like good music, that Sweet Soul Music?' I asked the disciples of the old California Ballroom in 1997. The California Ballroom had shut in 1980, but 17 years later, those disciples responded: 'Yes!!' That, among other things you will read in the book, was the birth of the Cali-R. Inside, you will also find pictures from the shows, and stories of major Soul acts who were the giants of our teenage years and who performed at Cali-R. These photos will mark the beginning of our events and take you right up to the events of this year, 2022. You will read about the experience of hundreds of people coming together to form a spiritual bond under the name of Soul Music.

Lastly, we speak about what the future holds for Cali-R and tie the beginning to the end of the book, which covers an event built on shared passion and love of music. Considering we have had 25 years of great, consistent Cali-R events, I wanted to celebrate them by sharing my experiences with you all and to offer more context and detail to anyone who has attended Cali-R and who loves Soul Music.

CHAPTER 1: *The Boy from the Bush*

Above: me on the right, aged 11, with a friend outside his flat in Shepherd's Bush. The scooter belonged to my sister's boyfriend

I was born on a fresh autumn day on 25th September, 1953, at Hammersmith hospital in West London, a stone's throw away from the famous White City Stadium, to my parents, Violet and Harry Hudson. This was the same time that the hit, "Look At That Girl" by Guy Mitchell, was No. 1 in the charts. Mum thought it was a sign, but instead, she got a boy, and little did she know that the connection she made to me and music was nothing to do with my gender but the start of my life-long passion for Motown, Soul and Reggae music.

Growing up, we resided on the fourth storey of a council flat in London with no lift. There were six of us in total: Mum, Dad, Joan (my older sister), John (my older brother), Mark (my younger brother), and me (Sid). While Dad was working hard, Mum used to carry all the shopping, the pram and us kids all the way to the top to reach our flat. She blamed the trek as the reason she had bad hips later on in life. I still think her bad hips came from too much dancing on the tables in the London pubs where she used to enjoy a Guinness and a good sing-song to local songs, such as "Maybe It's Because I'm A Londoner", in the 50s. Although we didn't agree on the cause of her bad hips, we did agree on our love for music and would often belt out a classic on our way up and down the four-storey stairs.

It was the mid-60s when I started to dive into music and artists, watching programmes like Ready Steady Go and Top Of The Pops. My brother and sister used to send me up to the record shop to buy records from the likes of Elvis Presley, Adam Faith and The Beatles.

When I was in the shop, I spent hours walking around, checking through all the records. I had so many questions about them, but back then, I was a bit too nervous to ask, so instead, I merely went to the counter to pay and then walked home. This pattern continued; instead, I answered my own questions by learning the name of almost every record vinyl in the shop, and sometimes bringing the questions home to my brother and sister. When I was about 12, my friends and I used to gather near the garages at night. We used to try to get near 'The Big Boys', as we called them. They were only 17 or 18, but to us, they were giants. We used to get as near to them as we dared to hear what they were saying. One of them, Peter Smith, had a Vespa GS scooter. Few people had vehicles in the flats, but the GS stood there as proud as a peacock, with the sunbeams hitting its highly polished chrome and mirrors, causing a kaleidoscope of images on the wall. However, The Big Boys didn't talk about the music I would buy for my brother and sister. They spoke of Tamla . . . whoever that was! They even mentioned Otis and Aretha . . . whoever they were! They talked about a John Lee Hooker, whom I thought was from the TV. I was shocked, as I hadn't heard of these people, and back then, you had no Google to solve your questions.

Some time later, I went back to the record shop for my sister, and a girl asked the manager to play "These Arms Of Mine" by Otis Redding. Otis sounded familiar, so I stood there and pricked my ears up in case it was the same guy The Big Boys were referring to. I was hooked from the first moment I heard this haunting, soulful masterpiece. It was like my inner passion for music was suddenly being connected to the evocative voice of this Soul legend. I wanted to hear it again but did not dare to ask. I could not afford to buy it, and the girl who asked to listen to the song purchased the only copy as Soul Music was not plentiful back then. As I walked home, I was trying to remember the melody in my head so that I could satisfy my fascination with some playback. For weeks, this number was in my head, and I was desperate to know more about the artist and the song.

Instead of buying sweets with the money from my paper round, I started saving up for records, and a year later, I returned to the record shop and bought Otis Redding's "Live At The Whisky A Go Go" for 17s 6d. I felt so proud, as this was the first record that I had bought with my own money, and I could finally sit and listen to the sound, which had tangled with my soul since I heard it a year previously, on my brother and sister's record player.

A month later, it hardly had any grooves left, as I had played it so many times. As I got older, I used to go to Shepherd's Bush Market on Saturdays looking for tunes; even in those days, it was very multicultural. I learnt so much about music by talking to people from the West Indies, Asia and Africa, and I loved these conversations, which gave me so much enrichment into other cultures and their music.

Money was quite hard back in the day, even though Dad worked hard, but fortunately, I had now also started working in a scrap metal yard. Therefore, I purchased my first stereo system on the never-never (hire purchase). The system consisted of a Garrard deck, Marconiphone amp and speakers paid for with a Provident cheque, which I paid back over many months. The quality of this equipment was amazing. I was enjoying life so much at this point. I had the music and the system, but being a peaceful skinhead, I only needed the sheepskin to complete the set. You didn't see too many sheepskins, even in London, as they were very pricey.

When I was about 16, I started going to The Boathouse Disco near Richmond for a dose of Soul and Reggae. The Caribbean community, who had come to the UK to create a new life, brought the Blue Beat, Ska and Reggae sound, which gave new life to an already exploding British music scene. I used to listen to Soul and Reggae up in the flats with my neighbour and lifelong friend Gary McCarron, who now lives in Australia with his wife Karen and family. That is where we practised our killer dance moves, which my sister later labelled embarrassing.

I'll take a step back to the sheepskin. I take after my good old Dad in liking the odd flutter. When an accumulator bet came in one Saturday, I purchased my first sheepskin, which became my pride and joy. I felt like going from the little boy who used to run to the record shop for his brother and sister at the weekend to one of The Big Boys who had a stereo, music, and now the sheepskin. Happy times for me.

When I was 17, we moved to Houghton Regis, as Mum and Dad were offered a council house. Mum never settled in Houghton, as she could never get over missing her friends or the London vibe. I started working at Waitrose supermarket in Dunstable, and it is unbelievable how many people who have come to Cali-R used to work there.

I soon became friendly with my life-long friend, Mick Monaghan. He told me one Friday: 'Come on, Sid, we'll go up to the California Ballroom.' I thought to myself: 'What is that?' Being from London, where you were served the best discos, nightclubs and live music scenes, for me, it was a first in many ways. However, I thought, whatever it was, it would be a good laugh. When I walked into the California, my jaw nearly dropped. The sound system was so crisp and clear. Lighting was so advanced that it took you on its journey around the hall. Although we had to walk there and back, we danced the whole night away and stayed almost every weekend from the beginning till the end. I attended the California Ballroom many times and saw many great artists. The atmosphere at the California was totally unique for the youth of Bedfordshire and beyond.

Above: the old California Ballroom

Around the same time, I was asked to DJ at house parties because of my stereo system and record collection. There was only one deck, but people were not in such a hurry in those days. This progressed, with me being asked to do weddings, birthdays in function halls and many more. After a while, I hired some equipment to make my bookings.

Next, to going to the California Ballroom, I used to visit The Greyhound. Their disco nights were Tuesday, Thursday and Sunday, but the music was more progressive – rock and charts. I remember taking "Here I Go Again" by Archie Bell to Mr H, the DJ. He played it and liked it very much. Then I brought a few more, which he played, and I got to know him well. His business partner Mick Parrott approached me at the Cali on New Year's Eve 1972 about doing a Soul night at The Greyhound. They wanted the music to be more diverse, as something would be on every night at the pub. In 1973, I started my first regular Soul gig at The Greyhound. Mr H christened me "Soulful Sid" that night. I was paid £3, and the taxi there and back was £3! I had to carry loads of vinyl, so going on the bus was out of the question. I changed my night at The Greyhound from Friday to Wednesday because I wanted to play more Northern Soul. I put an advert in Blues & Soul magazine, and the manager of The Greyhound thought he would have an easy Wednesday because not many people would come out. Unbeknown to him, the place would be jam-packed, and he had to get quickly on the phone to call in some more bar staff.

> **THE BIGGEST SOUL CRY IN THE SOUTH**
> **THE GREYHOUND**
> LONDON ROAD, DUNSTABLE, BEDS.
> **YOUR MAN AT THE WHEEL — SOULFUL SID**
> Playing sounds like
> Bob Relf, Tymes, Jerry Cook, Sweets, Tempos, Sam & Kitty, Rex Garvin, Inky Dinky . . . plus all the best of the best!

Above: Blues & Soul advert

I started supporting Mr H on some gigs, and thanks to him, I learnt a lot. He then got The Devil's Den gig at the California Ballroom. Devil's Den was a disco downstairs in the Ballroom. Mr H was a first-class DJ, but his Soul Music collection could have been better, and as The Devil's Den was all Soul Music, he asked me to join him with my records. I assisted him with the

Above: me starting the Soul night at The Greyhound public house, Jan 1973. This photo is courtesy of The Culture Trust Luton / the Luton News

music, and when I went on holiday, he said: 'For goodness' sake, make sure you leave me your box of sounds.' Mr H was part of the ESD Disco collective, which included Mick Parrott, Paul Belcher, Kenny and Stake. Paul was an electronics genius. He and the late Mick Ilka (Entertainments Manager at the California Ballroom) used to make sound equipment.

I purchased my first equipment, which they made. They tested the amp by throwing it off the top of the California Ballroom! The two speakers were oak and weighed a ton. Those speakers are still in my lock-up 50 years later and Paul Belcher, to this day, advises me on sound equipment. In 1975 Mick Ilka asked me to host a Northern Soul Night in The Devil's Den. Northern Soul was much more popular in the North of England, hence the title. The people who came to my gig were passionate and had great nights. The introduction of "Out On The Floor" by Dobie Gray still makes my body want to dance. It's all about the experience of being on the dancefloor and feeling like a king. Your soul is taken over by a rhythm that controls your body and makes you do things you thought you couldn't. As you read earlier on, music was always my passion. Becoming a DJ ignited my love for playing music and seeing people enjoy themselves.

I can't quite describe it, but when I stand in front of the crowd, the sensation of passion vibrates through my body, and I just play. If I had known when I was 12 how to turn that feeling, when I first heard Otis Redding, into action, I would have been DJing even back then.

Above: me, 1974, supporting Noel Edmonds at Dunstable College. Dunstable College was a great gig and myself and The Midas Roadshow had so much fun there

Above: Steve and Ian Ball of Midas Road Show, whom I fronted (great collaboration), supporting Radio 1 and TV star Noel Edmonds, at Dunstable College 1974

I used to DJ at the big colleges, with The Midas Road Show; also, at the Queensway Hall, Fridays Dunstable and others, many of which were private gigs. I remember doing a gig at Dunstable College in 1974, when Noel Edmonds was the show's star. We had a great night, and the place was packed.

At the end of the night, I was given my £6 and asked how much Noel Edmonds got. I was told about £750. I thought to myself that I really needed to put my price up. While DJing at the Queensway Hall, I met some young, fresh faces – The Real Thing. This was just before they debuted "You To Me Are Everything" but believe me, they were electric. In 1975, I met my wife-to-be, Jacqui, at Tiffany's. It was definitely the sheepskin jacket that convinced her to dance with me! Two years later, we married, and my second big passion in life was born when our three children – Brett, Brad and Darcie – came into the world.

CHAPTER 2: Birth of Cali-R

Married life was very busy, and a full-time job plus discos did not give me much time for me. Through the years, I met some really lovely people doing the discos. A few even adopted me as an extended member of the family. I got to know people all around Bedfordshire, and my week consisted of a full-time job, then out every Friday and Saturday night doing discos for a club or people's special occasions. When we had a chance Jacqui and I would go to London to see Major Soul Names. On one occasion we just finished a meal and was both walking towards the entrance of The Royal Albert Hall when a car pulled up. A guy started to walk towards the stage entrance. We couldn't believe our luck; it was Marvin Gaye strolling along on his own without a care in the world. We did notice he had some rather huge built friends in the car so we just said hello. I still to this day kick myself for not starting a conversation with him. On another occasion, we went to see The Jacksons at The Rainbow Theatre who were supported by one of the most hard working soul outfits - The Real Thing. They gave 110% and really got the crowd up for the main event. Michael Jackson had not yet gone solo but this magician had the audience lyrically and physically spellbound within 15 minutes of being on stage. We had great pleasure in watching the legend before all his trials and tribulations started. I thought to myself what I would give to put on a show like this.

In 1996, I got a phone call from a friend of mine – Rose Rafters, who lost her brother John in tragic circumstances. She wanted to raise money for his memorial garden, so she asked me to do a benefit night that year. Her request was for the whole night to be old California Ballroom tunes. This would be a gig that I would relish, given the format and my love for that style of music. The night was in St Mary's Social Club in Dunstable, and it was absolutely packed. It had been 16 years since the California Ballroom shut down, but this night brought together its old disciples who lit up the dancefloor, and it was a great event.

After the electricity this night created, I pondered on an idea to do another gig like it, as people missed the old California Ballroom nights. After some discussion with my wife and some creative brainstorming, I decided to put on a California reunion event to see how it would go. On April 5th, 1997, I put on the first California Reunion at The Gateway, Houghton Regis. I advertised it with one poster, in the old Plume of Feathers, Dunstable, which was run then by Joy and Jim Morris.

CALI-REUNION
Featuring ex. Cali DJ
Sid Hudson

Champagne quiz
Dance competition

Motown Soul Reggae
Memories
late 60's early 70's

Saturday 5th April
Gateway Hall
(above Somerfield)
Houghton Regis

7.30pm- Late

£5 Admission by ticket only

Left: The first Cali-Reunion ticket 1997

The tickets went fast, and they sold out before the date. I remember a phone call from Joy at about 6pm on the event day. She said: 'Sid, you are going to get mobbed tonight; everyone is talking about it.' The youth of Dunstable from the 70s had matured and were looking for an injection from the past to relive all those great memories. I had such a buzz in my stomach then, and all

I wanted to do was get to the event to feed the energy still circling around the area for a great night of Motown and Soul tunes. The night was electric, with non-stop dancing, and the chorus from the capacity crowd moved me very much. It felt like they were the orchestra, and I was the conductor.

After this night, I thought, well, that was a great night to remember the California Ballroom. I was considering doing another reunion, and people were ringing me and showing great anticipation for another gig. I couldn't believe it. I went away, gave it some thought and decided to book the Queensway Hall for a night in November 1997, thinking that if I were lucky enough to get 400 people, I would cover my costs. Three weeks before the event, I had sold 800 tickets. The Queensway Hall was a legendary building, like the California Ballroom, so it felt right to be staging it there.

Above: Queensway Hall. Photo courtesy of Geoff Cox. The Queensway Hall was a very well known venue in the entertainment world.
The Who, David Bowie, The Crusaders, Brothers Johnson are just a few Thousands of names that appeared there

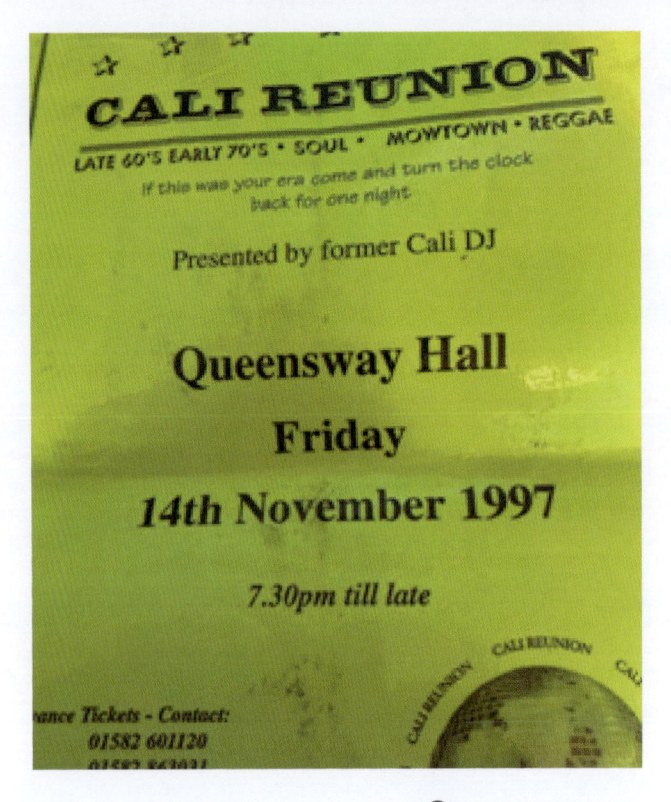

Left: Advert for 2nd Cali-Reunion 1997 which sold out 3 weeks before

This event was even better than the last one, with so many old faces turning up from everywhere. The tunes were being received with such affection from the audience, and the mood was just JOY! I got my old mate, Emperor Rosko, to send a taped message from the USA. That night "Bedfordshire's friends reunited" took place in the hall. There was no need for computers as people swapped phone numbers and put their arms around people they had not seen for years. This later extended to people, who had emigrated to all parts of the world, coming back for a trip and planning it around Cali Reunion to meet family and friends.

While still buzzing from the excitement, I went for a walk one day, trying to digest what was happening. I still remember being that little boy who heard Otis Redding for the first time and pondered over his music for weeks and weeks in my head. I always knew music lit up my inner passion, but to be able, now, to create and host something for people was beyond what I had ever imagined. During my walk, I began developing ideas in my head about how to enhance the event and magnify it even more for people. My next thought was, what about the stars who appeared at the old ballroom?

I came home and did some research. At the time, I thought Edwin Starr was the best of who was now available. I sat with my wife and began discussing the idea of hosting an event that would feature an artist like Edwin Starr. This was a big financial gamble for Jacqui and me, as we were now talking thousands, not hundreds, anymore. Jacqui did not doubt me and, with all her faith, told me she supported me, so I booked Edwin for February 1998.

Again, the ticket anxiety was there because, with live acts, they had to be more expensive. Well! What can I say? Two weeks before the date, it had sold out! Word was spreading about California Ballroom Reunion. When Edwin's band arrived on the day, he was still asleep on the coach. About an hour later, a funny feeling came over me; to go and see him, and as I walked towards the entrance, he came through. Straight away, he engaged in a conversation by taking a genuine interest in the gig. I told him it was a reunion for the California Ballroom. 'California Ballroom!', he replied, with a huge ear-to-ear grin on his face. 'That was my favourite gig back in the 70s,' he said.

'We are going to have some fun tonight.' That night started at 8pm, and by 8.30, the dance floor was packed with hundreds of people. The queue for the bar was ten deep, but nobody minded as there was such a feeling of togetherness among everybody. Edwin came on with his 11-piece band, and the crowd erupted, and for an hour, the audience was spellbound.

Above: Edwin Starr at Queensway Hall 1998. He was the first live act to appear at Cali-R. What a show!

Watching this master of Soul sing and dance his way through his catalogue, and other Soul classics, I felt proud and honoured to host this event. The lights were beaming, the crowd was on fire and I stood at the back watching with stars in my eyes. I slowly felt that shadow of a doubt I cast on myself fade into the music of the night. The Cali Reunion was not then, and is still not today, about me. I am proud to host it, but I consider myself part of a team of people who want to maintain and re-create a vibe, and stage what the old California Ballroom offered; where people could go and celebrate the power of Motown, Soul and Reggae. The Cali Ballroom had two floors, so that night, I asked ex-Cali Ballroom and Chiltern Radio DJ Louie Martin to join me, and then again at the next gig. Through the years, Louie and charismatic DJ Jellybean played the Jazz/Funk room upstairs at reunions, giving the gig the diversity of the old ballroom. The idea was to have a specialist room upstairs and the main hall downstairs.

Above: the crowd the night that Edwin Starr played the Queensway Hall for Cali-R, 1998

After this event's success, people demanded another Cali Reunion, so I contacted my old mate Emperor Rosko, in California, wondering if he would consider coming over to DJ. I doubted that he would, but he booked his flight that day when I told him what it was. At the fourth Cali Reunion, we hosted Rosko as the feature and a young man, Mr George Anthony, who had just won Stars In Their Eyes as Al Green. Rosko and George were both incredible. After the reunion, I met Rosko for breakfast at the Old Palace Lodge in Dunstable the next day. The night before, he had drunk at least a bottle of vodka while performing, but you would not have thought it because he sounded stone-cold sober. When we were at breakfast, my "full English" came out, and I said to him: 'Are you having one too?' He said: 'No, we are healthy in California; I don't eat that artery-clogging muck.' I told him: 'Charming! You don't eat this, but you sink a bottle and a half of vodka.' We both burst into laughter. Emperor Rosko, from the late 60s was my idol, and he certainly did not disappoint that night. Rosko and I have kept in contact over the years, and he sent me a wonderful voice note, which was played out at my 60th birthday party. I'm grateful my path crossed with such a true legend. You will see his picture on the first page of the next chapter.

Around October 1998, it was time for the next California Reunion, and this time, we decided to host The Drifters. At the same time, I decided that this was not going to be just a few reunion nights; this was something I wanted to carry on. Therefore, my wife and I decided to make it an independent night called Cali-R. The Drifters caused another sell-out, and the word about Cali-R kept spreading. We were having a great night, and at about 9.15 pm, The Drifters arrived. I was so keen to meet the legendary lead singer, Johnny Moore. To my shock, when Johnny climbed up three flights of stairs, he had to sit down for 15 minutes to recover. I was very concerned about whether or not he would perform. The minute Johnny had the mic in his hand, he turned into something else. From the side of the stage, I was virtually in tears watching this legend overcome his disabling illness to give a fantastic performance.

Phil, The Drifters' manager told me that Johnny wanted to perform for three more years, which would mark his 50 years with the group. I know it was Johnny's idea in the 70s to make the Drifters move to the UK because they were more popular here than in the US. Tragically, six weeks after performing at Cali-R, Johnny Moore passed away. Seeing him perform one of his last gigs with us was a privilege.

Aside from the iconic Drifters, a familiar name at The Cali-R. We also hosted . . . yes, you've guessed it: JIMMY RUFFIN.

November 1998, another packed house and the dancefloor was jumping with excitement and anticipation of another Motown legend. Earlier in the year, I had watched the outside broadcast of the Princess Diana tribute, during which Jimmy performed. I have to say, it sounded terrible, so I was slightly worried. When Jimmy came on and sang his first few chords, the sound man put his thumbs up, all his lights came alive and Jimmy was even better than in the earlier years. It was so funny to see two decades of a lot of the same ladies who used to scream and put their hands out at the old ballroom doing the same thing again. Still beautiful, though, I must add. It was definitely a strange type of déjà vu. The Supremes, Heatwave, Martha Reeves and The Vandellas, The Real Thing and Gwen Dickey (the voice of Rose Royce) all appeared at The Queensway Hall at our Cali-R events. When we had Martha Reeves appear, the company responsible for supplying their PA forgot to bring a bass amp for the guitar. The bass player rehearsed with the band for two hours, so they all sounded tight. It was a matter of waiting for his bass amp, which had to come from Manchester.

The bass player was a larger-than-life character, and when the amp showed up 30 mins before showtime, he said in his broad American accent: 'Shit! My grandson has a bigger amp than that in his bedroom'. 'I thought: 'Oh no! I hope it doesn't affect the show.' To our delight, it didn't, as he was a brilliant musician.

Unfortunately, after all these events, we were informed that another iconic building, the Queensway Hall, was due for demolition, so I had to find another venue. California Ballroom and the Queensway Hall hosted music royalty for decades. They sculpted many people's lives and contributed a huge part of the upbringing of Bedfordshire's teenagers. In the 70s, the youth didn't need to get into trouble through boredom or being led on. They were too busy enjoying the world-class acts that the little town of Dunstable used to host. When artists' tour dates were announced, people who were outside Bedfordshire would look at the national tour lists; London, Birmingham, Bristol, Manchester and . . .
 Dunstable. Dunstable? Where the hell is that? So many people in the UK, then, discovered Dunstable through these two iconic venues, and the memories created will live on in the minds and hearts, locally and nationally, for ever.

I searched for a new venue and decided to walk around the leisure centre in Dunstable. It certainly wasn't ideal, but it could work with much work and imagination. Everything had to be hired in; stage, PA equipment upstairs and downstairs, lights, bar and, because of the centre's schedule, we had to be dismantled and out by 5am sharp. Ladies were not allowed to wear high heels because of the floor, and there also were some smoking restrictions. Despite some of the hassles that came with this new venue, we made it work and hosted some great events there. In April 2000, Edwin Starr opened our new venue. Edwin once again performed a blinding show, together with his band. Edwin was a very sweet man. He knew his music wasn't in the charts anymore, so he looked after his fans. When they are finished, most artists will leave soon after their performance ends. Not Edwin; he would go and sit in the bar and chat with the people who came to see him. The numbers for the first Cali-R here were down, but George McCrae came next, and the numbers were gradually creeping up again. At that time, George lived in The Netherlands and Aruba, in the Caribbean, and he and his new wife, Yvonne, were just so charming. George didn't expect special treatment; he just went along with everything and did a wonderful job.

Then it was Ray Lewis with the New Drifters, and we were almost back to the capacity of 900. The fantastic Cali-R vibe won over people who were doubtful about going to a leisure centre.

The Cali-R was doing very well at Dunstable Leisure Centre, featuring Desmond Dekker and The Aces, Odyssey, Clem Curtis and The Foundations, Gwen Dickey, Heatwave, Jimmy James and The Real Thing, as well as Ray Lewis. In 2003, I took another gamble and booked The Stylistics, who were at a different financial level to the acts I had booked before. With a close eye on the box office, I saw the tickets fly out. The event sold out long before the night, and one of my ticket sellers was offered £250 for two tickets. The face value of the tickets was £44. He might have been tempted, but the thought of The Stylistics in Dunstable was something he would not give up on. A year after this event, Cali-R was featured on Anglia News, highlighting the reunion's success. Soon after this, I started doing Cali-R nights on a smaller scale; just me doing discos in Dunstable, Luton, Flitwick and Barton. These events were and still are very well attended today, and still sell out after all these years. We also have had a lot of successful outside events in the big marquee at Dunstablians Rugby Club, which has been very accommodating but, owing to development, cannot host Cali-R at the moment. Thanks to Paul and Janet Wallman, we had a great one-off outside event at The Fancott Arms, on the outskirts of Toddington, a few years ago featuring Joe Carter's Hitsville, The Sound Of Motown; 1,400 people partied the night away.

I continued with the bigger events as well, featuring top names. So many artists followed: The Fatback Band, Odyssey, Clem Curtis and The Foundations, Richard Street's Temptations and The Drifters. We have featured The Stylistics four times, as there was such demand; the last time in 2016.

The Stylistics in 2016 were the last act at the leisure centre before it closed for redevelopment and we moved our main events to Dunstable Conference Centre. The Community Church, as it is known, has been so welcoming. Julian Richards and his team have created a first-class entertainment/church venue. They have superb sound and lighting, and are eager to see our event go off without a hitch. Nothing is too much trouble, and they understand the art of putting on a show. The Conference Centre was an old cinema, making it perfect for a musical event.

Looking back over the years, I try to puzzle out the essence that actualised Cali-R's continuity, growth and success. Aside from the great team around Cali-R, I know it is down to our following, the people who come to the Cali-R; old members, new members and those who went to every single event, from the start right up until now. Sometimes I walk along the street and talk to people I have never met before, and they tell me stories about Cali-R; how they met old friends, new friends, partners or simply lived some of their best nights.

Some even now bring their children to experience the same night that their parents did at the old ballroom. Still, to this day, it ignites so much happiness inside me, and I want to express my gratitude to the people who come to our events. At the birth of a child, you have parents and a team of midwives and doctors to ensure everything goes to plan. However, when the doctors and midwives have delivered the baby and the parents have raised the child, you have the matured product in front of you, independently living and contributing to the world. Cali-R is the same; it was created out of love, delivered by a team of people, and now we watch a matured product that is a lifetime of memories and nights created by the people, which we will all carry with us for the rest of our lives.

In the next chapter, we will take you through photos of our events, from the first one to our most recent one. For some, it will be a chance to see the event in action; for others, it will be a trip down memory lane.

CHAPTER 3: *Photo chapter of Cali-R*

Left: me with Emperor Rosko at the Queensway Hall in 1998. When I asked him to come, he said: 'I suppose the reason they knocked the old California Ballroom down was because it couldn't take any more of that great Soul Music.' Rosko lived in Caddington in the 1970s before moving back to the USA

Left: Jimmy Ruffin giving the Cali-R crowd a big dose of Motown Magic in 1998 at Cali-R in the Queensway Hall. Jimmy, in the 60s, was on the verge of becoming the lead singer of The Temptations. He was pipped at the post by his younger brother, David. Jimmy went on to have a great solo career and moved to the UK in the 80s. He continued to perform and hosted a radio show. In 1984 he collaborated with Paul Weller on the song Soul Deep

Above: my two sons, Brad (left) and Brett (right), with Edwin Starr at Derngate Theatre, Northampton, 1998

Above: our amazing Cali-R crowd in dancing mood in 1999 at the Queensway Hall Nobody sat down it was just one continuous party. The venue had hosted thousands of big names and here was another one very soon to take the stage

Above: The Supremes, which included Freda Payne's sister Sherrie, cruising through the Motown catalogue in 1999, to the audience's delight, at the Queensway Hall

From Soul Boy To Soul Man

Left: 'Calling out around the World, are you ready for brand new beat?'… because now it's time to introduce Martha Reeves and The Vandellas

Right: Martha at the Cali-R, Queensway Hall, 1999. Martha had a great singing career and also went on to become a big voice in politics

Above: The Real Thing at the Cali-R Queensway Hall, 1999. These boys certainly are The Real Thing when it comes to performing. Chris Amoo's lead vocals capture your imagination instantly. Backed up by older brother Eddie and Dave Smith, The Real Thing never disappoint

Above: Gwen Dickey, the voice of Rose Royce, brought her show to Cali-R, Queensway Hall in 1999. She charmed the sell-out crowd and can be seen chatting with Jacqui Hudson

Above: me and the true legend who is Edwin Starr in 2000 at Dunstable Leisure Centre for Cali-R. On stage, his performance says it all. When Edwin comes off stage, you meet the nicest, warmest human being. He supports many causes and always has time for a chat

Above: Rose Rafters (sister of John, for whom we did a memorial night) in 2000 at Cali-R Dunstable Leisure Centre. Rose was regularly on stage at the old ballroom, dancing in competitions. Here she shows she hasn't lost her touch

Above: George McCrae. His wife, Gwen, was asked to record a song written by KC and The Sunshine Band. George was meant to be on backing vocals, but when Gwen was late, he recorded the song alone. The song was "Rock Your Baby", for which he was nominated for a Grammy. Dunstable Leisure Centre Cali-R, 2000

Above: Ray Lewis at Dunstable Leisure Centre in 2000. He was the lead singer of The Drifters for many years and brought his own special style to the Cali-R, where he was a huge hit. Ray can be seen here interacting with the crowd

Left: Mr Jimmy James at Cali-R Dunstable Leisure Centre, 2001. One of the country's true Soul pioneers, Jimmy always brings an array of talent with him. This, coupled with his masterful performance, makes a fantastic night. Some of Jimmy's fees had to be paid in cash. For some reason, he only asked for it a short time before he went on. When the time was right, I told Jimmy it was time to go on. He said to me in a jovial voice: 'See that lady counting the money? That's my wife. I am not going on till she is finished!'

Above: Luton Town legend Ricky Hill with Gwen Dickey, 2001

Left: Mr Clem Curtis appeared at Cali-R three times. He was a joy to know, a pleasure to listen to and even more fun to watch. This photo was taken at Cali-R Dunstable Leisure Centre in 2002

Right: Cali-R favourite George Anthony warming up for Jimmy James at Cali-R Dunstable Leisure Centre, 2001. On the balcony, you can see my two sons and two of their friends proudly watching

Top Left : Desmond Dekker, Cali-R Dunstable Leisure Centre, 2002. He performed an extra 30 minutes at Cali-R, such was his respect for his audience. He started with his Jamaican No. 1s and then followed with a string of his UK hits. Desmond remembers the old Cali Ballroom. He told me: 'We always finished the tour there because it was so good.' Desmond loved Cali-R, but he said; 'Next time, I would prefer bigger heaters in the dressing room, Sid. I was freezing, man.' Sorry, Desmond! The following year I was responsible for putting Desmond Dekker in at the Luton Carnival, where there was an array of Caribbean food and wonderful sunshine. When I asked Desmond and his manager what food they wanted, they replied: 'Fish and chips!' Although surrounded by food, we had to drive to the fish shop to get them what they wanted. I said to Desmond: 'At least it is a bit hotter here than it was at my gig last December, Desmond.' He laughed

Above: Jack Saunders and Denis O'Donoghue backstage with local legends RDG at Dunstable Leisure Centre Cali-R, 2002

Left: The Stylistics say thank you to the Cali-R audience after giving them 75 minutes of pure vocal perfection. This was Cali-R Dunstable Leisure Centre, 2003

Above: The Stylistics returning a year later to the delight of Cali-R fans. Arrion Love and Herb Murrell are original members and still sound as good as they did all those years ago. This photo was taken at Dunstable Leisure Centre Cali-R, 2004

Above: Pleased to meet you, Sue! Sue Pringle travelled from her home in New Jersey, USA, via Nottingham to pick up her brother, Steve. He had arranged a special night for her at Cali-R with friends and relatives. Sue had moved abroad from her home in Tithe Farm Road more than 30 years ago, and this was the first time she had returned. This photo was taken at Dunstable Leisure Centre Cali-R, 2004

Above: Sally Parris and Jacqui Hudson with The Stylistics, 2004

Above: In 2005, the Cali-R was the launch pad for Diane Ilka's book, The Cali Album, which was very successful. In this photo are far left: Denis O'Donoghue, Sally Parris, me, Louie Martin and JB. Front from the left, Jacqui Hudson, Diane Ilka and Clem Curtis. Dunstable Leisure Centre, 2005

Left: Danny, Doug, John and Martin enjoying Cali-R Dunstable Leisure Centre, 2005. On the next page you will see them in 1976

Above: the same four at the Cali in 1976

From Soul Boy To Soul Man

Above: are you ready to do the Bus Stop? The whole floor was doing it when The Fatback Band came to town. Dunstable Leisure Centre Cali-R, 2006

Left: the preparations for a Cali-R taking place here at Dunstable Leisure Centre, 2006. Everything had to be dismantled after the show to ready the leisure centre for opening at 5am

Above: Geraldine's 50th birthday. She's pictured here receiving a bottle of champagne from the Stylistics' Herb Murrell. Dunstable Leisure Centre Cali-R, 2007

Above: Jim and Chris pictured with Marvin Ruffin (Jimmy Ruffin's cousin) at Dunstable Leisure Centre, 2007. They have been coming to Cali-R since it started

Above: Geno, Geno, Geno! Oh yes, quite simply brilliant! Geno had a huge following in the 60s and 70s, but not having hit records, his popularity dwindled, so he moved back to the United States. Then came Dexys Midnight Runners' "Geno", which relaunched him in the UK. Geno has been performing here ever since. This was Cali-R at Dunstablians Rugby Club, 2008

Right: Dunstable Leisure Centre Cali-R, 2010 with Richard Street's Temptations. Street was a member of The Temptations for more than 25 years. In the early years, when Temptation Paul Williams was struggling with an illness, Street used to sing the words off stage, and Williams would mime. Eventually, Street became a full-time member. He brought his Temptations to the Cali-R, and the audience sang along to all the classics, including My Girl, Get Ready, Ain't Too Proud To Beg. What a night that was!

Above: some Cali-R fans meeting Richard Street's Temptations at Dunstable Leisure Centre, 2010

Left: a 2011 section taken from Dunstable Gazette – Lynn Grady rolled back the years and the miles to see The Drifters perform at Dunstable Leisure Centre on Saturday night – 38 years and 10,000 miles, to be precise. Lynn, who lives in Gold Coast, Queensland, Australia, with her husband Shaun, last saw the legendary pop and Soul band perform at the California Ballroom when she was 15 and was determined to see them again when she heard that they would top the bill at Sid Hudson's Cali-R Christmas Special, travelling 10,500 miles in the process

Above: The Drifters in 1973 at California Ballroom. Lynn is somewhere in the crowd. This photo is courtesy of the Luton News

Above: Drifters, 2011, at Cali-R Dunstable Leisure Centre

Above: thanks to Paul and Janet Wallman, 1,400 people descended on The Fancott Arms, near Toddington, for an open-air special. The miniature railway was hijacked to become "The Soul Train" as people clambered on for a ride while listening to top tunes. Joe Carter's Hitsville, The Sound Of Motown, took to the stage and left the crowd begging for more at the end of their set. This was Cali-R at The Fancott, Toddington, 2013

Top (Left): Cali-R Christmas Special, Dunstable Leisure Centre, 2014. Father Christmas (Ron Horniblew) and Ian Philpot

Top (Right): Cali-R Christmas Special, with Angelo Starr and The Team. Dunstable Leisure Centre, 2014

Bottom: Odyssey Going Back To Their Roots with a classic performance. Dunstable Leisure Centre Cali-R, 2015

Left: Brett Hudson and Ryan Ambury preparing for Cali-R, 2016

Below: The Stylistics, 2016. Dunstable Leisure Centre Cali-R

Above: it's that special time of the year. Christmas Cali-R Dunstable Leisure Centre, 2016

Above: some of the bar staff are ready for a busy night!

Above: Clem Curtis celebrated his 76th birthday with his guests, The Flirtations, at the Dunstable Leisure Centre Cali-R in December 2016. It was such a happy night, with The Stylistics topping the bill at the Christmas Special and I conducted 900 people as they raised the roof with a fantastic Happy Birthday To You for Clem. He came up to me just after and said: 'Thank you so much, Sid. That was really kind, but I missed it -- I was in the toilet!'

Above: what a nice day for a party. Dunstablians Rugby Club, 2017

Left: we are here to greet you – New Year's Eve, 2016

Below: (left to right) Mick McGrath, Colin Watts, me, Gill Sollenberger, David Sollenberger and Ian Philpot. Gill and David planned a trip to Cali-R from their home in Barbados. They both had a great time with family and friends at Dunstablians Rugby Club, Cali-R 2017

Above: what a legend! Dunstablians Rugby Club Cali-R, 2017

Above: Dunstablians Rugby Club Cali-R, 2017

Below: Andy on a trip to UK from his home in Australia. He leaps onto the stage and then conducts the whole show with his voice. Ripper Mate! United Services Club 2017

Above: Julie celebrates her 60th birthday with family and friends at a Cali-R Summer Festival. Dunstablians Rugby Club, 2017

Left: Looking good, feeling good. Dunstablians Rugby Club, 2017

Above: Summer Festival in full swing, 2017

Below: the IT girls at Dunstablians Rugby club, 2017

Above: Suzanne, one of our long-term supporters and her lovely friends. United Services Club, 2017

Below: every floor needs this brilliant dancer

Above above: nice to meet you, girls. United Services Club, 2017

Left: there is dancing, and there is this brilliant mover!

Above: what a vibe with our Cali-R crowd at United Services, 2018!

Below: Ray Lewis with two lovely ladies at Cali-R Dunstable Conference Centre, 2018

Above: Angelo Starr continues on from his late brother Edwin. Angelo packs a powerful 90-minute set. Christmas Cali-R Dunstable Conference Centre, 2019

From Soul Boy To Soul Man

Right: Diana Baker on her trip over form Australia

Below: Dunstable Conference Centre Cali-R, 2021. It looks like you're enjoying yourselves, ladies!

Above: I can only keep this smile for so long. Dunstable Conference Centre, 2021

Left: Dunstable Conference Centre, 2021

From Soul Boy To Soul Man

Above: smile girls. Dunstable Conference Cali-R, 2021

Below: our door ladies are ready to greet you!

Top: let the good times roll! Cali-R Dunstable Conference Centre, 2021

Bottom: Our delightful, supportive, positive energy bombs – Tina Mckay (left) and Lynn Jarrett, enjoying the Cali-R Dunstable Conference Centre, 2021. Tina and Lynn support in running the bars

From Soul Boy To Soul Man

Left: take a breather, guys, you'll be back on the dancefloor soon!

Below: the Party People at Cali-R Dunstable Conference Centre

Above: dance like nobody's watching, ladies!

Above: Cali-R Dunstable Conference Centre, 2022, with The American Four Tops

Above: left to right, the fantastic Elizabeth Davies, Alan Adair and Alan Davies in July 2022, at Dunstable Conference Centre. These three met during the COVID Mixcloud live streams without knowing that they had been three of our most loyal Cali-R supporters and had been coming to the events for years and years

Left: come on, boys, show us how it's done

Above: waiting for The American Four Tops Dunstable Conference Centre, 2022

Below: 25 years of the Cali-R taken in July 2022 at Dunstable Conference Centre, left to right, Darcie Hudson, Jacqui Hudson, Isabelle Dudley and Colin Dudley from Three Star Coaches

From Soul Boy To Soul Man

Posters of Cali-R Events

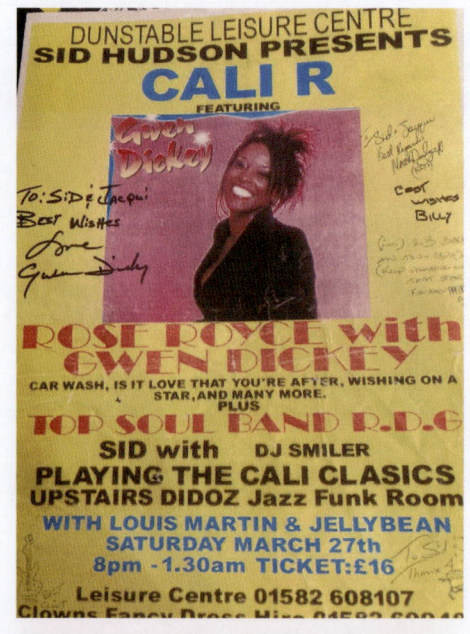

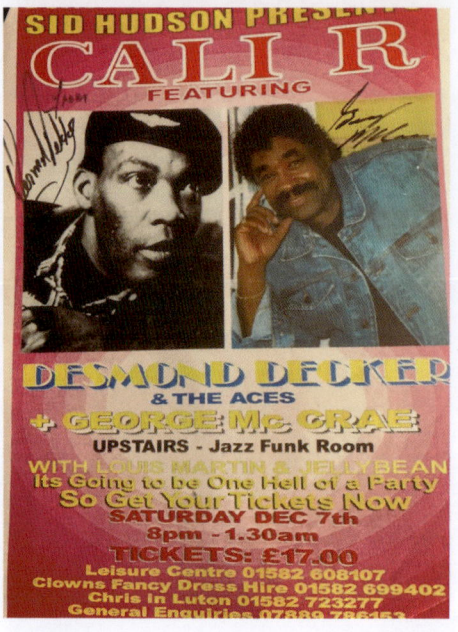

Sid Hudson

Posters of Cali-R Events

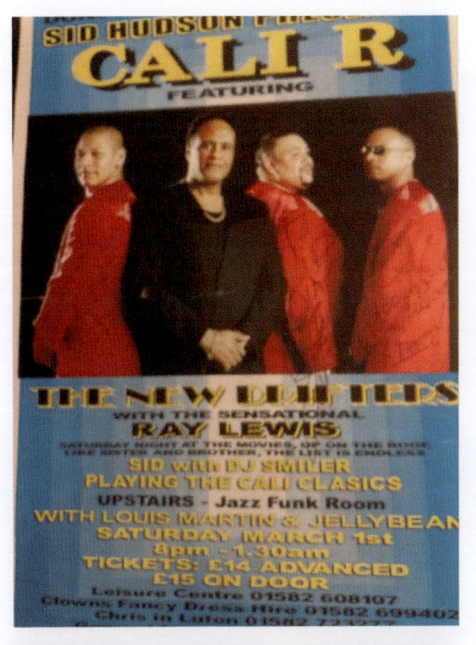

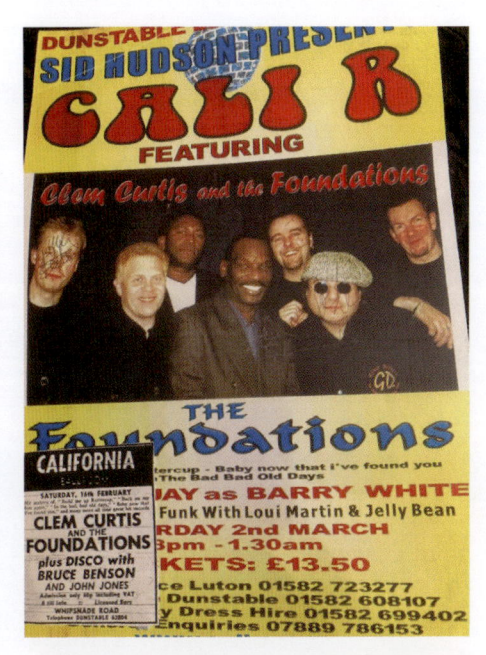

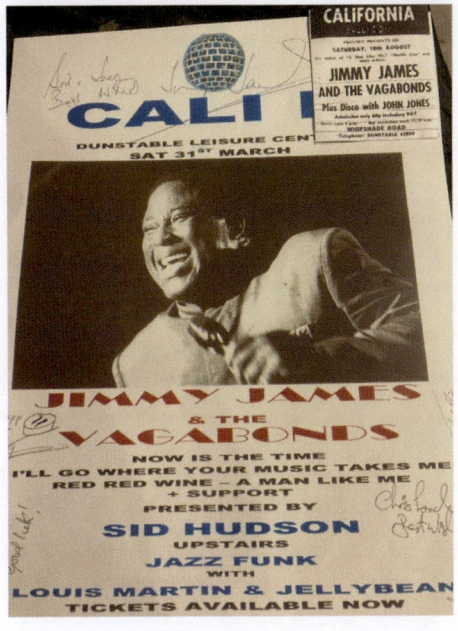

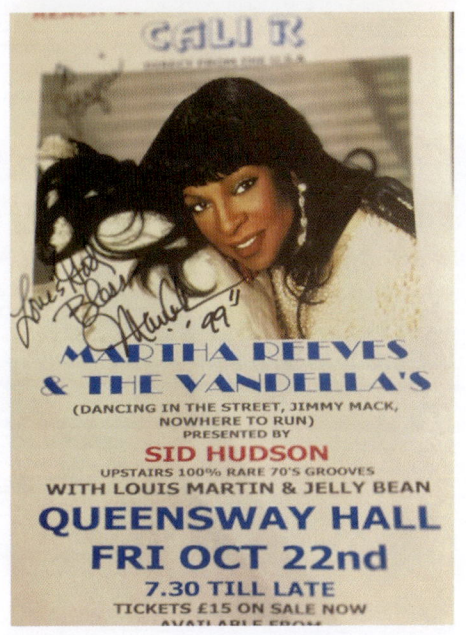

Posters of Cali-R Events

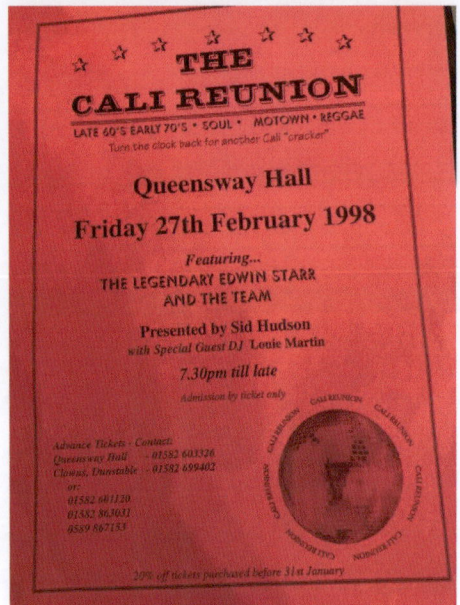

Above: left to right: John Dunn, Jacqui Hudson, Kath Gill and Julie Dunn. This photo was taken at United Services Club, 2022. John and Julie have been attending the Cali-R since it started

We have many more photos of the artists, crowds and events that we would love to share. These photos can be found on our Cali-R Facebook page, which you can find under the name Cali-R (California Ballroom Reunion). Sorry if we missed anyone out; it was definitely not on purpose.

CHAPTER 4: Life Around The Cali-R

Cali-R is an event enjoyed by so many people. It is a night where old friends, new friends, artists and the Cali-R crowd come together to enjoy. There is so much work that goes into the event. However, it has not just been the moments at the event that have made Cali-R what it is but also all the efforts, memories and moments around it. In this chapter, I would like to thank a few people who have kept Cali-R going and made it what it has been over the years. I would also like to name a few special moments around Cali-R, including the Cali-Ballroom sign at Royce Close, Dunstable, our two awards and the COVID-19 lockdown Mixcloud Cali-R specials.

Dedications and thanks to the people around the Cali-R, past and present:

Jacqui Hudson – My wife. She has supported me from day one. She has not only believed in me but has also seen me through thick and thin. Jacqui has made suggestions and ideas that we have implemented throughout the years.

She has also been present at every event on the door, offering guests a warm welcome. The performers always like Jacqui a lot. I remember when she hit it off with Rose Royce star Gwen Dickey. Gwen was headlining our event in 2007, and Jacqui complimented her on what a lovely bag she had. 'Yes,' Gwen said, 'this is Armani. It was given to me by one of my promoters.' Jacqui said: 'Sorry, Gwen, the only thing we can offer you is a Tesco bag!' Gwen erupted in laughter and said: 'You are so funny, Jacqui!'

Brett Hudson – My son. He has been a huge driving force from the age of 13, when he first started helping to put the show on. His cool head and no-panic attitude in a crisis have saved us several times. Brett is responsible for putting on the bar at big events and helping to put on the show. When I had a disabling illness a few years ago, Brett ran the whole show, supported by Jacqui, Darcie and Brad. Brett will solve any logistical problems, however hard. Brett now runs his own very successful business but always finds time for his Dad's events. Thanks, Brett

Brad Hudson – My son. Although living in Australia, Brad regularly contacts me with ideas and things he has seen to enhance the Cali-R.

Thanks to him, many people in Sydney now know about Cali-R. Brad runs his company from Sydney

Darcie Hudson – My daughter. Darcie is such a powerful weapon to have in your arsenal when putting on events. Her communication, advertising and presentation skills are critical to sustaining the event. Darcie lives in The Netherlands and runs her own successful recruitment company with her boyfriend, Erwin, but her commitment to Cali-R is full-on. Also, I would like to thank her for helping me to write this book. Without her creativity and dedication, I couldn't have done it

Ian Philpot – From day one, Ian has committed himself to Cali-R. Ian's late mother, Mildred, used to run the charity raffle in the early days. Mildred would also make up the mailing list. Ian has worked continuously: the official photographer, distributing flyers, selling tickets, preparing the hall for events, running artists about and much more. Every successful event needs an Ian

Erwin Rozeboom – We call him the Flying Dutchman because he flies over and helps us at every big Cali-R event. Thanks for all your ideas, help and commitment, Erwin

Above: my wonderful family. Jacqui is on the far left, Darcie next to her, Ian (Adopted Uncle) in the middle, Brett next to Ian (Adopted Uncle) right side, Brad far right, and me all the way in the back.

Left: my lovely son-in-law Erwin Rozeboom left with Jacqui Hudson right

Denis and Anne O'Donoghue – Denis has repeatedly put his expert skills as a journalist to use in covering Cali-R events, while Anne was so supportive while working on the Dunstable Gazette. Den is always there to help, to advise, to make the events go smoothly. His musical knowledge has been a great help when called upon

Mick and Marie Monaghan – We have been friends for 50 years. They are the kindest, most genuine people you could ever meet. Mick would always drop everything if I needed something doing at Cali-R. He regularly fitted the soundproofing in the leisure centre, among other things. Thank you both

Jack Saunders – Mr Encyclopaedia Dunstable. If it's about Dunstable, or 60s and 70s music, and Jack doesn't know, then it is not important. Jack's record collection would make the keenest collectors' eyes water

George Anthony – For multiple stunning Cali-R performances over the years

Tony Orouke from Orourke Media

Above: from left to right Denis O'Donoghue, Mick Monaghan, Jack Saunders

Geoff Cox and John Buckledee – Former Luton News/Dunstable Gazette editors, for their generous coverage over the years. This trend has been continued by Steve Sims and Bev Creagh in the Luton News

Don Neufville – For featuring Cali-R in his weekly column in Dunstable Gazette multiple times

Singers Mick Walker and Clayton Stevens – supporting the main act

Louie Martin – Louie was a big name at the old Cali Ballroom and went on to have a successful radio career, coupled with live gigs. He was on the line-up on the famous Knebworth Soul All-Dayer. Louie can be heard today on Solar, the premier Soul radio station

JB – Jellybean started with Louie in the Jazz/Funk room from the beginning. He plays only vinyl, and his unique style has made him a favourite with the crowd

Lynn and Tina – Loyal supporters of Cali-R since Day One. They have helped in various roles and are the backbone of our bar staff

Sally and Ian Parris – They have played an influential role in Cali-R over the years and have always been there for us. Ian started off running the security at Cali-R, while his lovely wife Sally, a treasured friend, worked very hard with the admin on event nights. Thank you both

Nic Gorgone – Nic took over from Ian as head of security, and his expertise helped Cali-R to run smoothly

Alison Creigg – Alison helped us for many years and greeted people at the ticket desk with a warm smile

Alex Storey and Stacey Brinklow – Alex is a hit with the ladies and is always willing to lend a hand at Cali-R events. Stacey sometimes manages the bars and has always helped us and stood in if needed. Thanks, you two

DJ Smiler (Paul Hodges) – Paul was very supportive in supplying equipment and lighting. Paul helped me on the decks a few times, and his musical knowledge was excellent

Colin Watts – Colin has played the Jazz/Funk room in the past few years at Summer Festival. He owns Bluebird Records, and his popular show is on Diverse FM weekly.

Mick McGrath – Mick has always been supportive and supplied equipment for big events

DJs Duncan Bedford and Dave Grimes – Thanks for all the Summer Festival sets

The two Sharons from Don't Let Dunstable Die – You

have always greatly supported Cali-R and aided its path. Also, Bev of About Dunstable

Dunstable Conference Centre team Julian, Olly, Ricky, Dan and Vic – Thank you so much

Roberto Giacobbe (former Ops Manager DLC) and Debbie Taylor (former Manager DLC) – Two people who made life easier for Cali-R while it was at Dunstable Leisure Centre. Many thanks for the commitment of these two gems

James Ellershaw, and previously Sally, at Dunstablians Rugby Club – Thank you for your total commitment to Cali-R

Audrey Tyler, Eugene and Kirsty Ghent, Keith Wellings – Always showed such commitment when I have used their marketing services

Michelle Anne – Another diamond who made putting on events at United Services Club so much easier with her professional, energetic attitude. Thanks to Jo from United Services as well

Andy Chesham – Andy is very supportive of Cali-R and is a great DJ promoter and friend

Hilary Garrard – For all her help with advertising distribution over the years

Mick Radford – We swap anxieties and moan together like two old gits

Tony Randino – Thanks for all your help

Ellen at Perfect Print – Thank you

Wayne and Kevin, DSC Sound and Lighting, Dunstable

WF Security – Special thanks to our incredible security team from WF security. The guys are thorough, always turn up and have become people we love to work with

Barry Collins Entertainment – fantastic service over the past 25 years

Maureen Turner from Barton Village Hall - thanks for all your support and partnership

Ryan Ambury & Ryan Woodbridge – thanks for all your help over the years

Samuel Groves our charismatic photographer

Left: Left to right - some of the WF security team. Jake Riches, owner Wayne Fuller, Maxine Fuller, Gary Fuller

Memorial Day

The old California Ballroom was the heartbeat for Bedfordshire youth in the 60s and 70s. Although the building was knocked down in 1980, the tens of thousands of memories locked in the minds of the people who attended the events will never, ever be demolished.

Dunstable was a small town, but when it came to entertainment, it featured some of the biggest national and international stars. I was very keen to get a road sign to mark the place where this colossus once stood. I campaigned to the council, and they agreed the place should be marked with a sign.

The sign was erected at the Royce Close site of the old Cali. Following this, we organised a special day to mark the fitting of this sign and a tribute to the California Ballroom. We invited both former owners of the old ballroom, the Green and Ilka families, and a marquee, with photos and complimentary drinks, was erected.

The event was covered by Three Counties Radio DJ Martin Coote, who gave over his whole three-hour show to the project. Many people were keen to air their stories about the old ballroom. Cali-R features the disco 70s era of the Cali, but I am well aware it flourished for ten years in the Swinging 60s. It was lovely to hear people's stories about The Rolling Stones, The Who and many more.

Cedric Green, son of Edwin Green, who built and opened the California Ballroom, said publicly how delighted he was to see his father's work commemorated. Diane Ilka was equally impressed and was gathering information for her forthcoming book, The Cali Album. People exchanged many stories about the old place, and all had a joyous day.

Above: The Original California Ballroom sign
And below the sign to Commemorate the Cali Ballroom & Pool. Pictured members of Green & Ilka family, Sid & Jacqui Hudson former Cali DJs and Council officials

Above: My lifelong friend Gary checking on the sign I was responsible for at Royce Close

Book signing Russ Sainty(King of the Cali)

In the autumn of 2009, I was asked by Paul Bowes, then the owner of The Book Castle, Dunstable, to put on a celebration night for the signing of singer Russ Sainty's King Of The Cali book. Some big names from the 60s, including Brian Poole and Pete "Peanut" Langford from The Barron Knights, whom Russ invited, plus Cedric Green and his family, came along. Russ, at this time, was in his 70s but still gave a memorable performance for all his old fans. Two of Russ's old bandmates from The Nu Notes, Mel Miller and Bernie Martin, were also there. Russ told me that he and The Nu Notes headlined the old Cali 338 times in the early 60s. On one occasion, the support band were late, and when they arrived, they all looked scruffy and did not need a dressing room. Russ told them: 'I will do a couple of numbers and give you time to prepare.' The support band were eventually ready and went on. Russ told them: 'I'll be back to do my headlining set.' The support band came on, and the place went wild. He had to go on for his set but knew it was pointless because of the support band's effect. The support band that night was: The Rolling Stones.

Mixcloud and our online streaming of Cali-Rs during lockdown

Well, a couple of years ago, we had COVID, and everything was shut down. The world was a bit upside down and full of uncertainty. The family discussed doing something, as we all missed holding the events and seeing our Cali-R crowd. People had supported us for 22 years at that point, and now it was time to return the favour.

Thanks to this idea from Brett, we started streaming live Cali-R music sets on Facebook every Friday and Saturday night from 8pm. Word spread, and hundreds and then thousands soon joined us. It was important to pay tribute to the people on the front line fighting this invisible enemy and let them know we were behind them. We had people logging in from the USA, Australia, New Zealand, Canada, Japan, South Korea, Iran, Iraq and continental Europe. My wife Jacqui would dance while I talked and played the tunes. She soon became known as "The Dancing Queen". Facebook was unhappy about our streaming on their platform, making it impossible to continue. I then had to find another way to host the show. Jamie Horton stepped in from his home in Ireland and spent countless hours of valuable free time getting me set up on Mixcloud, the British online music streaming service, as I am a bit of an old fart when it comes to new technology! Jamie was then and still is a star. The shows were a great success for more than a year. We heard stories about old friends reuniting, people making new friends and generally how the shows helped many people to get through lockdown. When Friday night came, many people would get dressed up, log in, pour themselves a drink, connect the show on their TVs and have a boogie around the living room or kitchen. It also got us through lockdown as, once again, the Cali-R crowd showed that their united force could get through even the most difficult times. As the world is slowly getting back to normal and we can see people again, we do a live stream every few months and have returned to our regular, in-person events.

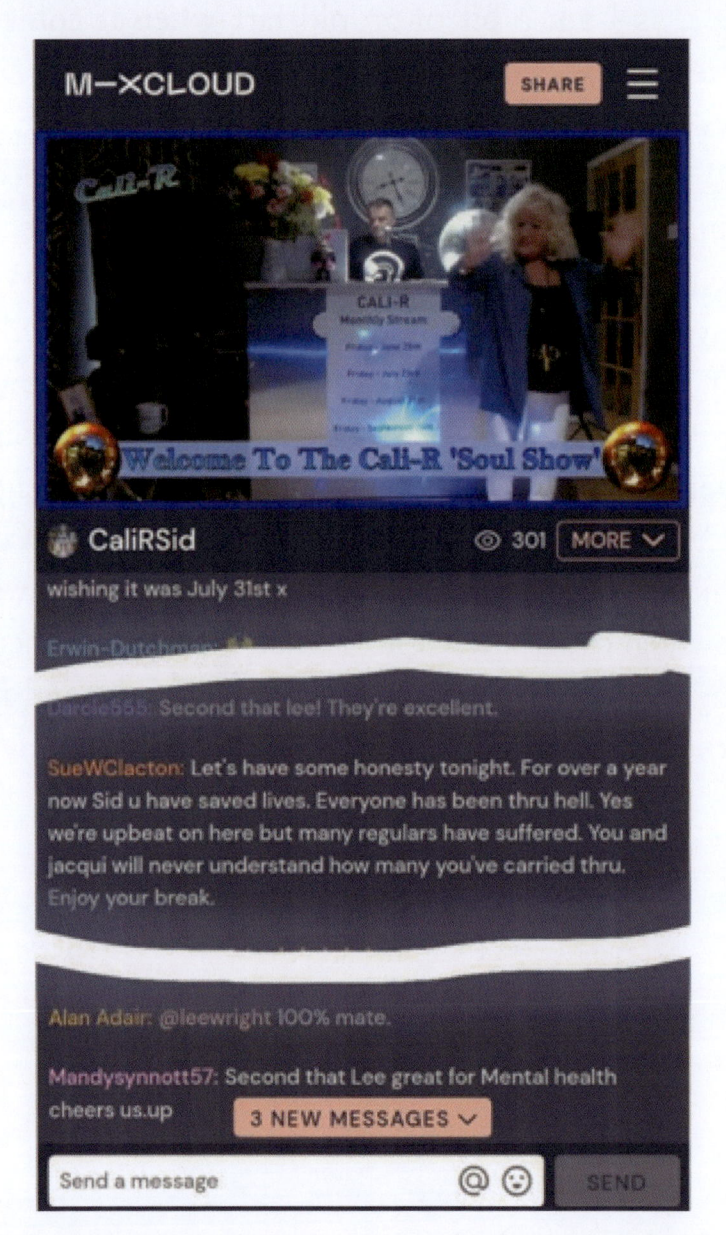

Above: Our live mixcloud set on screen and one of the many wonderful comments we received from our Cali-R crowd. During Corona, we all came together, and I will never forget the magic or strength we all created. Thank you to everyone who joined us

SME Business awards 2021

While doing the live Mixcloud shows, our listeners nominated us for the local (Bedfordshire) SME Hero Award. Owing to the number of votes we received, we ended up winning the gold award, which was unexpected and incredible at the same time. Scoring gold meant that we automatically qualified for the national awards, and we went to Wembley Stadium in The Bobby Moore Suite in July 2021. There, we won the silver award for National Business Hero, handed to us by Paul Farmer, the CEO of MIND. This was again totally unexpected and one of the proudest moments of my life. I want to take this moment to thank sincerely every person who nominated and voted for us. It was not about winning the award, but the feeling it gave us, knowing that we could give back to people during one of the most testing times in our 21st-century history. Cali-R Mixcloud during COVID was an organic, unplanned branch of Cali-R history, but it will go down as one of the most rewarding, pleasurable and synergistic times in our 25 years. Thank you, everyone.

Left: Right to left, me, Jacqui holding the gold award and Brett at the Bedford Corner exchange.
Right: Right to left Darcie, me, Jacqui and Erwin outside Wembley stadium, holding the silver national business hero award

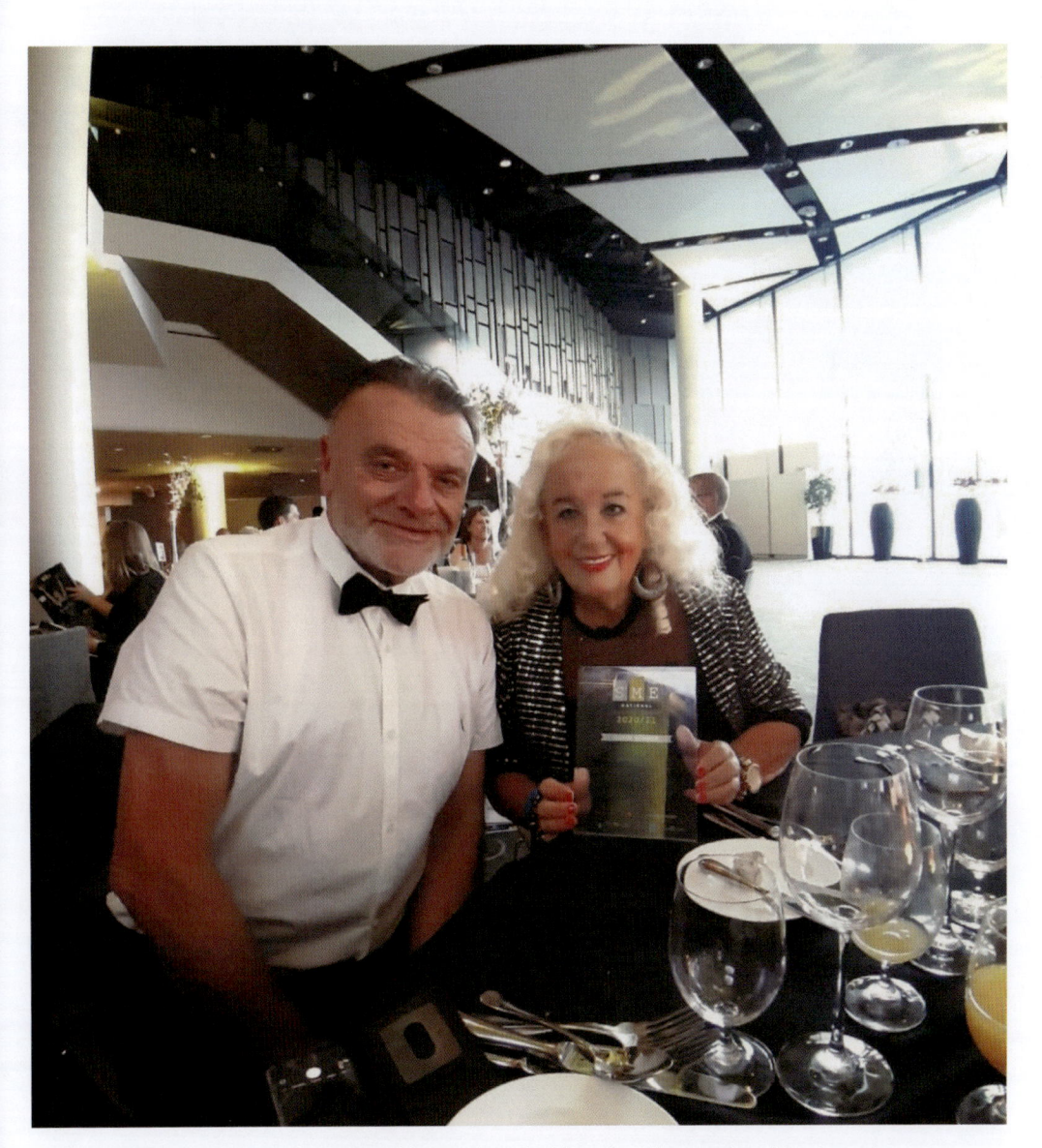

Above: Jacqui and I at Wembley stadium holding the silver national business hero award

From Soul Boy To Soul Man

Above: Alex Storey Left to right, Ian Philpot (second from left), Brett Hudson (third from left) and Ryan Woodbridge (far right).

Left: Mick and Marie Monogahan

CHAPTER 5: Cali-R Going Foward

Up until now, we have taken a look back at Cali-R. We have taken it back to how it started, reminisced on the incredible memories, illustrated some picturesque moments and remembered some of the times around Cali-R history. This year, 2022, marked 25 years of Cali-R. It is hard to believe that the event for us is still as electrifying and uniting as when it first started, but that is down to the team of people and the crowd who kept it going.

Many people have been asking me what is next for the Cali-R. Two-and-a-bit decades of memories, but what does the future hold, Sid?

Looking forward, I see the Cali-R going on for as long as I draw breath. We, as a family, have had so much pleasure in putting on the event for all these wonderful people. When you look at a Cali-R gig, you always see everyone smiling. It is the people's event, and they have come to form a community for one night, where they reach out and touch the past. They draw on the energy of their youth and keep the dancefloor full all night.

The spirit of Soul Music ignites their passion and takes them back to a time when nothing mattered.

We are planning an outdoor event for next year (2023) and will feature events in more different areas than usual.

We will always use the venues where we have performed in the past, but we're always on the lookout for new ones to keep things fresh.

There is an old saying that if you have to ask what Soul Music is, you will never appreciate it. Soul Music is a feeling that fills your body with different emotions. When dancing, the spirit controls you and works through your body, orchestrating your dance moves.

When listening to Soul Music, it touches your heart and soul, taking your mind on a journey while listening to the message it sends. The music originated from slavery, when people had no rights or possessions. They were, however, rich with the spirit of the Gospel. It brought them together, and they sang and worshipped to form an unbreakable spirit. Soul Music is a collective where people, despite race or religion, come together and rejoice in the music they love.

It's been my great honour to play the music I love and spread happiness to many people over the years.

From the little boy who first heard the moving beats of Motown and Soul Music, to the man who raised my family around it and crafted a Cali-R which commemorates music and the old and new youth of our era, I always acted from passion. My biggest advice to anyone reading this book is always to follow and do what you love. Life will change along the way, but your passion will always stay close to who you are and what you do. When you act from passion, it will ignite energy inside you, and one day, you may also be a 69-year-old man looking back on a path of your own fruitful invention; where you see people dancing in the streets, sincere friendships that reach out and are there, artists who really know how to go out on the floor, unplanned bumps that get better with time and the best of my love; which has been my family and Cali-R. That is, where the power of music and passion collided.

To the Cali-R crowd, the team, the venues and my family – from the bottom of my heart - thank you all for this amazing 25-year journey. We cannot wait to share with you what is next.

To the people who have not been to our events yet, the question is: do you like Sweet Soul Music?

Come and join us for our next event!

Printed in Great Britain
by Amazon